Leopards

Leopards

Mary Ann McDonald

THE CHILD'S WORLD®, INC.

Published in the United States of America by The Child's World®, Inc.
PO Box 326
Chanhassen, MN 55317-0326
800-599-READ
www.childsworld.com

Product Manager Mary Berendes
Editor Katherine Stevenson
Designer Mary Berendes
Contributor Bob Temple

Photo Credits
© 1999 Anup Shah/Dembinsky Photo Assoc. Inc.: cover
© 2000 Anup Shah/Dembinsky Photo Assoc. Inc.: 19, 20
© Daniel J. Cox/naturalexposures.com: 13, 16
© 1994 Fritz Polking/Dembinsky Photo Assoc. Inc.: 9
© 2001 John Warden/Stone: 26
© 1995 Kevin Schafer: 30
© 2001 Manoj Shah/Stone: 2, 6, 23
© 2000 Mary Clay/Dembinsky Photo Assoc. Inc.: 10
© 1992 Stan Osolinski/Dembinsky Photo Assoc. Inc.: 15
© 2001 Stuart Westmorland/Stone: 29
© 2001 Tim Davis/Stone: 24

Library of Congress Cataloging-in-Publication Data
McDonald, Mary Ann.
Leopards / by Mary Ann McDonald.
p. cm.
Includes index.
ISBN 1-56766-886-0 (library bound : alk. paper)
1. Leopard—Juvenile literature. [1. Leopard.] I. Title.
QL737.C23 M35 2001
599.75'5—dc21
00-010771

On the cover...

Front cover: This leopard is keeping an eye out for danger as it rests in an African tree.
Page 2: This beautiful female leopard lives in the Masai Mara Game Reserve in Kenya.

Table of Contents

A herd of deerlike impala stand drinking at an African water hole. Suddenly, one impala jerks up its head. It snorts a warning call, and the herd comes to attention. Within seconds, the herd runs away. What scared the impala? A big spotted cat walks quietly out of some tall grass. What is this animal? It's a leopard!

⇐ This female leopard is stalking an animal in the tall grass nearby.

Where Do Leopards Live?

Leopards live in more areas of the world than any other big cat. Leopards are found in many parts of Africa, southern Asia, China, and Korea. They live in rain forests, jungles, mountains, grasslands, and even cities and towns. They roam from sea level to the highest mountains.

This young female lives in a rock cave in Kenya. ⇒

What Do Leopards Look Like?

Like other cats, leopards have long bodies, big paws, whiskers, and a long tail. Adults can grow to be eight feet long and weigh more than 200 pounds. But the special thing about leopards is their spots. Most leopards are tan with many dark spots. The spots help the leopard hide. This type of protective coloring is called **camouflage.** Some leopards that live in thick jungles are black, with spots that are very hard to see.

Leopards are shy animals. They are mostly **nocturnal,** which means they are active at night. They like to hide in trees or bushes during the day. Many people who go to Africa never see a leopard because these animals are so hard to see in the daytime.

How Do Leopards Hunt?

Leopards are **predators,** which means that they hunt and kill other animals. Leopards hunt by quietly sneaking up on, or **stalking,** an animal. Leopards can't run very fast for very long. They must be close to an animal to catch it. Sometimes a leopard waits patiently for something to walk by.

A leopard attacks by leaping from its hiding place and using its front legs to knock the animal down. The leopard grabs the animal's throat and bites down hard. Unable to breathe, the animal soon dies.

Here you can see this adult leopard as it ⇒
stalks its prey in some tall grass.

What Do Leopards Eat?

Leopards are **carnivores,** or meat eaters. They hunt and eat birds, monkeys, small mammals, and larger grass-eating animals. They also eat insects and reptiles when they are very hungry. Leopards that live in cities eat dogs and stray cats. Occasionally, leopards eat people. That only happens when there is no other food for the leopard to eat.

This adult in Africa has caught a monkey for dinner. ⇒

A leopard hangs its food in a tree so other animals won't eat it. The leopard grabs the neck of the dead animal in its mouth. Using its claws and powerful front legs, the leopard climbs the tree headfirst, carrying the kill. This food will feed the leopard for several days.

⇐ This leopard has brought her kill up into a tree. You can see it behind her.

Do Leopards Live Alone?

Leopards are **solitary** animals, which means that they like to live alone. Each leopard lives in a large home area, called a **territory,** that it marks with its own smells. The only time leopards get together is to mate. Three months later, the female gives birth to one to three babies, called **cubs.**

This leopard is marking its territory by scratching a tree. ⇒

What Are Baby Leopards Like?

Leopard cubs are born blind, deaf, and unable to walk. Their mother hides them for the first six weeks. She uses caves, hollow trees, or thick bushes to hide them. It is a dangerous time for the cubs! The mother must leave them for several hours each day while she hunts. The cubs drink their mother's milk when they are small. After about three months, they start eating meat.

⇐ Here you can see a young cub as it plays near its mother in Kenya.　21

The young cubs play and learn to climb trees. They follow their mother and learn to hunt. The mother leopard walks with her tail curled up and held high. The cubs see her white-tipped tail and follow her. Even in tall grass, the cubs don't get lost.

Leopard cubs stay with their mother for about two years. Even after they start to live on their own, the mother leopard helps them find food for several more months.

This older cub stays near its mother as it watches ⇒
other animals across a field in Kenya.

Do Leopards Communicate?

Leopards communicate in many ways. They mark their territories by spraying their scent on bushes. Other cats smell this and know who lives in the area. Leopards also use their bodies to communicate. They twitch their tails, arch their backs, or lay back their ears. Other leopards understand these signals and stay away.

Leopards make many sounds. They grunt, growl, snarl, and hiss. Young cubs meow for their mother. Leopards also make a special sound when they want to be heard far away. This call is a rasping cough that sounds like someone sawing wood.

⇐ By pulling its ears back and curling its lips, this adult is showing that it is angry and wants to be left alone.

Do Leopards Have Relatives?

The *clouded leopard* and the *snow leopard* are close cousins to the leopard. The clouded leopard lives in Southeast Asia's rain forests. It climbs trees to hunt birds and monkeys. The snow leopard lives in snowy regions of Asia's Himalaya Mountains. It eats mountain sheep and smaller animals called marmots.

⇐ From close up you can see that this snow leopard has thicker fur than a normal leopard.

Do Leopards Have Enemies?

Leopards have many enemies. Baboons, lions, and hyenas attack baby leopards. These animals also kill adult leopards if they get the chance. Enormous snakes called pythons also eat leopards.

For leopards, like many other animals, the greatest enemy is people. Leopards almost died out, or became **extinct,** when people hunted too many for their beautiful spotted coats. Laws have now stopped most of the hunting and helped save these big cats.

This leopard is curious about the photographer's camera. ⇒

Are Leopards in Danger?

Many of the world's wild cats are in trouble. Some are still hunted for their beautiful coats. Others are losing their **habitat,** or living areas, to people who are building cities and roads or using the land for farming. Luckily, the leopard has hope. It can live in many different places and eat many different things. With help, leopards will survive. Then we can all enjoy one of the world's most exciting wild cats.

⇐ This young male is resting before going out to hunt in Kenya.

Glossary

camouflage (KAM-oo-flazh)
Camouflage is coloring or markings that help an animal blend in with its surroundings. A leopard's spots act as camouflage to help the leopard hide.

carnivores (KAR-nih-vorz)
Carnivores are animals that eat other animals. Leopards are carnivores.

cubs (KUBZ)
Baby leopards are called cubs. Mother leopards give birth to one to three cubs at a time.

extinct (ek-STINKT)
An animal becomes extinct when there are no more left alive. Overhunting almost caused leopards to become extinct.

habitat (HAB-ih-tat)
An animal's habitat is the type of environment in which it lives. Leopards have lost much of their habitat to farming and building.

nocturnal (nok-TUR-null)
Nocturnal animals sleep during the day and eat and roam around at night. Leopards are nocturnal.

predators (PRED-eh-terz)
Predators are animals that hunt and kill other animals. Leopards are predators.

solitary (SOLL-ih-tayr-ee)
Solitary animals prefer to live by themselves. Leopards are solitary.

stalking (STAW-king)
Stalking is following and sneaking up on a person or animal. Leopards hunt by quietly stalking other animals.

territory (TEHR-ih-tor-ee)
A territory is an area of land that an animal claims as its own. Each leopard has its own territory.

Web Sites

http://www.africat.org/ (Be sure to click on "Predators in Africa.")

http://www.primenet.com/~brendel/leopard.html